Energy Healing Business

Trains the Mind
to
Attract Money

This document is geared towards providing exact and reliable information in regards to the topic and issue covered. The publication is sold with the idea that the publisher is not required to render accounting, officially permitted, or otherwise, qualified services. If advice is necessary, legal or professional, a practiced individual in the profession should be ordered.

- From a Declaration of Principles which was accepted and approved equally by a Committee of the American Bar Association and a Committee of Publishers and Associations.

The information provided herein is stated to be truthful and consistent, in that any liability, in terms of inattention or otherwise, by any usage or abuse of any policies, processes, or directions contained within is the solitary and utter responsibility of the recipient reader. Under no circumstances will any legal responsibility or blame be held against the publisher for any reparation, damages, or monetary loss due to the information herein, either directly or indirectly.

Respective authors own all copyrights not held by the publisher.

The information herein is offered for informational purposes solely and is universal as so. The presentation of the information is without a contract or any type of guarantee assurance.

The trademarks that are used are without any consent, and the publication of the trademark is without permission or backing by the trademark owner. All trademarks and brands within this book are for clarifying purposes only and are the owned by the owners themselves, not affiliated with this document.

Table of Contents

Introduction

Before we begin, I would like to thank you for purchasing the book "Energy Healing Business: Trains the Mind to Attract Money." I hope you find this book informative, helpful and a good read.

Are you familiar with the concept of energy healing? If you are, did you ever consider the potential of it in your life? Even if you are a skeptic when it comes to the main principles of energy healing, did you know that it could help you attract wealth? I bet that caught your attention quickly and fear not because it is true. There is a lot that humans know, but the unknown is a much more vast area to explore. It is a given that no person can know everything even if they spent all their waking moments reading a new book.

If you accept this and keep your mind open, you will have opportunities to learn a lot in your lifetime. Energy healing falls under this category of the unknown for most people. This book will help you understand so much that you might not even have thought of before. However, once you have finished, you will realize the true potential of energy healing. Another thing to consider is that according to a lot of studies, the law of attraction does hold true. This principle applies in your life in so many ways. A lot of us tend to complain about what happens in our lives or the hardships that fate throws at us.

Most people believe that they don't have any control over the experiences they have in life, but this is not true. As a human being, you can choose what you want to experience. You can also choose the experiences that you want to avoid in your life. While this has a positive aspect, it can also be negative. People tend to block out anything that they don't understand or necessarily like. This can prevent growth and inner peace on various occasions. In this book, we will focus on the positive aspect of it all and show you how to harness the energy and attract wealth and happiness into your life. So keep an open mind and be ready to explore beyond what you already know.

Chapter One : What is Energy Healing?

The human body resembles powered batteries that use the energy from Earth and the Universe to revive. Earth allows us to heal and also gives us all that we need in order to endure all hardships. It works with the Universe to associate with a spiritual energy that keeps our bodies functioning every single day. There is a steady flow of energy from the bottom to the top of our bodies. An energy healer trusts that with this progression of vitality, the body can mend itself under normal circumstances. We are altogether comprised of tissue, blood and bones. Be that as it may, the physical body is only the start of the story. Centuries ago, Traditional Chinese Medicine (TCM) acquainted the people of old with the meridian system and the energy chakras. Present day science (over the most recent 100 years) tells us that everything is comprised of energy.

Medicinal professionals additionally recognize the advantages of energy healing. As per a 2007 overview, 800 clinics in the United States have started to utilize Reiki, a prominent type of energy healing.

If they are unblocked, energy fields make it simpler to center and keep up an uplifting viewpoint on life, which will urge the body to re-establish itself to a state of normal health and wellbeing. There is solace in realizing that the people of yore and present-day science are both right.

People are, at their core, constantly vibrating in special electromagnetic waves. All physical medical issues, emotional aggravations, and financial troubles are related to imbalances in energy. Most individuals are encountering stress in life because of their hectic and demanding way of life. This causes disturbances in the body and can prompt physical issues like sleep deprivation and emotional swings. More individuals are starting to understand that they can see positive changes by concentrating on energy healing.

According to energy healers, all medical problems begin on an energy dimension with a stressor that can obstruct the progression of energy. Emotional and mental burdens are enormous blockages to our own development and growth as an individual. This blockage can work its way into the body and causes an aggravation, which can prompt significant medical problems. As people, it is our job to deal with our energy-body just as we do our physical body to ensure this doesn't occur. With the assistance of energy healing, these energy levels can be cleared, enabling us to achieve our maximum capacity to lead a happier more beneficial existence with more inspiration and strength. The mind is an incredible thing and thoughts are associated with the spirit and the physical body with a direct connection. One approach to clear these energy blockages is to relinquish every single past injury and negative connection. On the off chance that you hold on to the majority of your negative encounters throughout everyday life, at that point, your body will react in a negative manner. So it's ideal to accept every day as it comes, work through the majority of your feelings, and realize you are another you every day you wake up. By keeping your mind in a stable state, you will ensure that your body will follow the same pattern.

One of the greatest advantages of recuperating naturally is that it enables everybody to improve themselves and have a superior existence. When you are thoroughly adjusted, you are more inclined to remain positive and see life from an alternative perspective. This uplifting viewpoint averts misery and enables the body to unwind and maintain harmony, tending to potential issues before they form into an energy blockage.

Another approach to remove these blockages is to work with a Reiki professional, who will channel the energy of the Universe and pass it along to you. Reiki energy goes where the body needs it most, and it can provide a few solutions to get to your correct energy stream. We'll clarify how this functions and what you can expect from a treatment session in this guide. Meditation is additionally another great way to figure out how to detect your blockages in energy, purge what is needed, and evacuate the block yourself. A healer can likewise detect these energy barriers remotely and help you figure out how to clear them.

Talking about your nature, energy healers who are trained well can see auras and decipher their hues. They separate it for you and relate this to the soundness of your chakras. Open and adjusted chakras can improve things greatly. Crystal healing can enhance the positive energy, invigorate your energy stream, and even repulse negative vibrations. You will get acquainted with an assortment of crystals for healing and learn their properties as you learn more about crystal healing. Some of the popularly used crystals are amethyst, tourmaline, rose quartz, jade and clear crystals.

Energy healing is a kind of treatment that controls the energy circuits in your physical body to help encourage the body's repair systems. This comprehensive methodology is incredible for aiding the healing procedure by unblocking the energy fields, and it to avoid future issues by identifying them before they transform into any form of the disease in our physical body. By tending to the energy of your body, you will improve your overall wellbeing and attain more mental clarity.

Chakra harmonizing, crystal healing and Reiki are only a couple of approaches to advance energy healing and keep up an internal harmony. While not a substitute for counsel from an individual doctor for the physical body, these techniques help you make a quicker, simpler recovery by getting you in contact with your spiritual body. One ought to dependably counsel their doctor for any physical illnesses. These holistic practices work by rebalancing the body's energy and clearing the energy fields. By working in a straightforward manner with the energy, this impacts everything from mental, spiritual, to physical prosperity.

The practice of energy healing isn't governed by any laws. It doesn't require state or government permitting or any kind of all-inclusive authorizing. In any case, numerous energy healers do have proficient accreditations and have been trained in explicit kinds of healing.

Numerous energy advisors and healers have considerable experience with alternative medication. Physiotherapy advisors, attendants, and instructors regularly wind up attracted to the energy work callings. It's not surprising that numerous energy healers may likewise be authorized, medicinal specialists.

In the event that you are keen on consulting an all-encompassing energy healer, you ought to ask what strategies and modalities the expert uses and if they have any accreditations or expert certifications. It would be smart to question precisely what the session involves. The trust and solace factor is particularly significant in distance healing, even more than in-person sessions.

Chapter Two :
History of Energy Healing

Various cultures around the world have studied energy healing for many centuries. Reiki is the Japanese custom of energy healing, and it goes back to the mid-twentieth century. Chakras are the seven energy transmission centers found in the body and are portrayed in ancient Hindu writings. Meridians, the energy superhighways of the body, are the guides on which customary Chinese drug experts have based needle therapy or acupuncture. Albeit different antiquated societies utilized various modalities to invigorate the body's current capacity to recuperate, they all observed inner energy as an amazing power of good. Most of us have learned in secondary school science class that all matter is comprised of particles. No matter how solid and firm something looks, for example, a table, it is constantly vibrating. As people, we, as well, are vibrating.When you state somebody has "great vibes," you are truly discussing that individual's vibrational energy — upbeat individuals vibrate on a higher recurrence.

You can feel their bubbling energy! Places have vibes as well. When you stroll into a room in which people have recently fought, or something has recently happened, you may feel a deep dark energy that makes you want to leave immediately. The shoreline has a light vibe because of the salt (a natural energy chemical) and moving air. The air at the shoreline vibrates at a higher recurrence too. You know that you don't have to comprehend the law of gravity before you can fall down, similarly you don't have to totally get a handle on the idea of energy healing before you jump into the training. I would suggest running in with a receptive outlook for the greatest advantage.

It is always a good and appropriate time to visit an energy healer. On the off chance that you are pushed, on edge, or physically depleted, an energy healing session can enable you to unwind and feel better. Furthermore, in case you're now feeling better, it's constantly conceivable to improve even further! Note that energy healing is an integral methodology that shouldn't prohibit any Western prescription you might take. There are a wide range of different types of energy healers, and you can discover them for all intents and purposes all over the place. There are Reiki professionals everywhere throughout the world, and the benefit of Reiki healing is that it tends to be given and got regardless of whether the customer and expert are in a room together or not. Why? The intensity of it makes energy stream to where it's generally required. Acupuncture therapy specialists are also available in most places; however, the people who undergo this treatment should be in the physical nearness of the needles. It cannot be carried out via distance healing. This methodology allows the movement of chi to rebalance the body.

Reflexology is another method that opens up blocked energy and advances the process of recuperation by invigorating the meridians, organs, and various systems via the centers on the person's feet, hands, and ears. Indeed, even massages are an energy healing practice, for they help to discharge pressure in the muscles, energize the movement of lymph, and allows profound relaxation. Get a referral for a respectable specialist in the event that you are new to these practices — you can ask at a yoga studio or ask an acquaintance who's into alternative healing. Beginning with a concise 30-minute session of Reiki tells you how groundbreaking energy healing can be.

Similarly, as you shower and brush your teeth consistently for body cleansing, energy purification is likewise an everyday duty. When you meet an energy healer, keep the positive vibes streaming by washing up in pink Himalayan or Epsom salts for 15 – 20 minutes. Do this whenever you begin to feel the negativity crawling again into your body. Smirching, or burning sage around you, likewise clears negativity from your surroundings. Positive energy crystals have their own healing properties and can help give your energy field a lift.

All you need in order to start your energy-healing venture is interest and an eagerness to learn. Who knows? You may very well get snared into it forever!

According to research conducted by quantum physicists amid later years, a lot of light has been shone prominently on the extraordinary effect that the intensity of the psyche has on our lives and the universe as a whole. The more that this thought is investigated by researchers and incredible masterminds alike, the more prominent an understanding we have on exactly how noteworthy a job the psyche plays in molding our lives and our general surroundings.

It doesn't make a difference in the event that you absolutely never come to have a thorough comprehension of the quantum physical science behind the Law of Attraction. In any case, this does not imply that we as a whole can't appreciate the numerous advantages that this liberal law can offer us.

As physicists come to supply us with increasingly more data in regards to the law, the more we can just cheer in the genuinely freeing and engaging acknowledgment that we are the makers and controllers of our life and the energy we are altogether made of. Be glad, for the universe is definitely on our side! The more time you commit to figuring out how to utilize the Law of Attraction viably, all the more satisfying and remunerating your life can be. There are no limitations! Open your psyche and appreciate the natural abundance in the Universe.

How Do You Like The Book So Far?

<u>LEAVE FEEDBACK ON AMAZON</u>

<u>If you're undecided, just leave a review later...</u>

Chapter Three :
Law of Attraction

Basically, the Law of Attraction is the power to attract things we desire or are focused on achieving in our lives. They say that paying little mind to age or religion; we are on the whole defenseless to the laws, which administer the Universe, including the Law of Attraction. It is the Law of Attraction that exploits the power of the mind to interpret whatever is in our thoughts and emerge them into the real world. In essential terms, all contemplations transform into reality in the long run. On the off chance that your thoughts are centered upon a negative fate or agony, you will stay under that haze. In the event that your thoughts are centered on positive outcomes and you have objectives that you mean to accomplish, you will figure out how to accomplish them with huge determination.

This is the reason the universe is such a vastly amazing place. The Law of Attraction ensures that whatever can be envisioned and held in the inner being is reachable as long as you make a move on doing what needs to be done in order to get to where you need to be.

The Law of Attraction is one of life's greatest riddles. Not many individuals are completely mindful of the amount of influence the Law of Attraction has on their everyday life. Whether we do it intentionally or accidentally, we live as human magnets that convey our thoughts and outlooks and attract a great deal of what we give.

Sadly, despite everything we are heedless to the potential that is bolted profound inside us. Thus, it is very simple to leave your musings and feelings unchecked. This conveys the wrong thoughts and pulls in increasingly undesirable feelings and occurrences into your life.

Having said this, finding the Law of Attraction is working away nonstop inside your life ought to be an extraordinary reason for celebrating! When you have comprehended the intensity of it, it is never again a mystery. In addition, you will have figured out how to apply these to your regular day to day existence viably; hence your whole future is yours to make.

The most testing part of recognizing and tolerating the reality of what the Law of Attraction brings to the table is going to be the acknowledgment that each and every one of your choices throughout everyday life, great and awful, have been formed by only you. For some, this can be a harsh pill to swallow, particularly in the event that you feel that you or your friends and family have been given some especially hard blows throughout your life.

In any case, when you have really come to comprehend the genuine key behind the Law of Attraction you will be reconnected with the staggering knowledge that you are allowed to assume responsibility for your life and free yourself always from the cycle of dread, stress or antagonism which has kept you down for a really long time.

The Law of Attraction truly is that straightforward. All laws of nature are totally immaculate, and the Law of Attraction is no exemption. Regardless of what you are hoping to have or accomplish or be throughout your life, in the event that you can hold on to a thought and see it for yourself in the inner consciousness, you can make it yours to have with some exertion on your part.

Chapter Four :

Using the Law of Attraction for Money

Was the possibility that you could draw in wealth one of the primary things that attracted you to the Law of Attraction? Provided that this is true, you're not the only one. Nearly everybody needs to discover how to draw in more money by utilizing the Law of Attraction systems. Nonetheless, perhaps you've now found that strategies to pull in cash are more befuddling than you anticipated. On the other hand, maybe you think you've been doing all the correct things however you haven't exactly made sense of how to utilize the Law of Attraction to gain wealth.

On the off chance that you need to realize how to build wealth as quickly as possible, first, you have to ace some simple activities. We'll create a layout of these activities below, and furthermore, investigate how to attract wealth rapidly and effectively by utilizing focused energy on reflections to draw in riches. In the end, we'll take a gander at the best intentions for money. Before you know it, you'll be prepared to manifest anything in a matter of seconds!

At times, specialists have stated that you can manifest anything you want in 7 days. In the event that the procedure hasn't been as straightforward for you, at that point you may be enticed to surrender your Law of Attraction work.

In any case, it's totally conceivable to manifest riches! You need to procure the correct methods. Moreover, regardless of whether bounty is your principal objective, you'll unquestionably profit by pulling in more cash into your life in any case.

Regardless of whether you need to go out on the town with your fantasy partner, begin another business, venture to the faraway countries or assemble your confidence, some additional money can't hurt. In a considerable amount of the best Law of Attraction cash stories, financial achievement is the portal to an enormous number of different types of accomplishment. Things being what they are, there is no reason not to spend the following week or so sharpening these idiot-proof strategies.

Usually, among the top of Law of Attraction cash tips, this activity is predicated on the central Law of Attraction premise that you draw in a greater amount of what you center your thoughts around.

In this way, if you tend to invest more energy concentrating on the wealth you have, more could come your direction. There are numerous approaches to do this. For instance:

You could keep a diary and make an everyday habit of taking notes on 1-5 things you're thankful to have. Remind yourself what you're grateful for. Close your eyes for 3-5 minutes, investing all the energy you possess on your most profound sentiments of appreciation for the bounty in your life.

When you're endeavoring to pull in bounty, your internal tendency to find faults will regularly convince you that you can't. Here and there, it will even disclose to you that you don't have the right to be well off.

At whatever point a negative idea like this emerges, promptly flip it around and center upon the opposite. For instance, when you stress, "I don't think I'll ever be sufficiently efficient enough to make a profit," immovably let yourself know "Everybody can be sufficiently successful and make profit."

In the event that negative energy creeps in, utilize an idea halting method like stating, "Stop" for all to hear or imagining a red stop sign.

One more ideal approach to pull in cash is to guarantee you spend the riches you have on things that truly matter. When you live in a manner that lines up with your values, you get a lot of joy from spending and build up a considerably more positive association with cash. What's more, when you see the cash in a positive manner, you'll draw in more cash right away!

What's more, in case you don't know what you esteem, do these:

1. Record the five most significant encounters of your life.

2. Compose five words that portray each of those encounters.

3. Ask yourself: what basic topics develop? These are your key qualities.

The manifestation of riches isn't just about associating wealth with satisfaction. It's additionally about taking a gander at the truth of your money related circumstance and acting in the appropriate manner. In this way, be straightforward with yourself. Observe all your funds, and keep in mind your obligations. Try not to be hesitant to ask for help on the off chance that you need it. Companions, family, and money related consultants would all be able to enable you to attract up an arrangement to improve the circumstance.

In the event that you don't have wealth today, that is alright. Advise yourself that it's impractical to get to where you need to run except if you align it with the reality of where you are at this moment.

While it may sound abnormal at first, you'll be better at utilizing the Law of Attraction for cash and riches in the event that you connect with the smell of money. When you do this, you adjust your own vibration to riches and bounty. As you do this, envision yourself as having all the riches you need. Try not to consider why you need cash, or how you wish you had more cash. Give your mind a chance to trust you are completely inexhaustible at this moment. This is a fast and simple exercise. Nonetheless, done regularly, it can reset old negative convictions about money, ones that are keeping you down.

Numerous individuals incidentally cause self-damage. In this way, you may in some capacity fear what will occur in the event that you pull in a lot of wealth!

Record every one of the reasons you may be reluctant to be copious. For instance, you may express "Imagine a scenario where individuals just use me for my riches?" or "What if I'm emotionally disturbed regardless of how rich I am."

For each fear that you have, consider where it originates from. Did somebody from your past give you this message? Is it originating from your social setting? Note the source.

At long last, find a solution to each stressful cause. For instance, "Despite everything, I'll know genuine companions from false companions regardless of how well off I am."

Chapter Five :

Energy Healing Tips for Prosperity

Many energy-healing tips are used in different parts of the world to attract wealth and abundance. The following tips are very effective and can help you further in your journey to attract abundance. Familiarize yourself with the various reiki symbols mentioned here and begin practicing these on a regular basis. You will observe real positive results much sooner than you ever expected.

1. The dollar symbol tip is easy but quite effective every time you spend money or even sign checks, draw the dollar image on some part of the note or check and give some Money Reiki to it. You can pray and state that any person that receives that money will be honored with bounty and bliss in their life. It can be unrealistic to do this every single time you are using a separate note or check. However, you can carry this Reiki out on a bunch of cash and checks together and keep them ready. At the point that you spend the cash or give a checkout, say thank you to the money for helping you in your life. This simple practice will create a positive cycle that will encourage cash flow in your life. No matter how much you spend, it will help to enhance the amount that comes back to you in multiples of what you spent.

2. The manifestation symbol can be made in two different ways. One way is to take some paper and note down what you need in terms of finances and draw the symbol of manifestation on all the four corners of that piece of paper. Now keep this paper in your desire box and offer Reiki to it every single day till your desire is fulfilled. Another way to do this is envision what you want inside a chi ball and give it the image of the manifestation symbol with CKR. Send this to the universe and ask the universe to help you in fulfilling whatever your desire is. Practicing this on every new moon will help you attract abundance all the time.

3. Get a nice wooden box that you like or make a little box at home utilizing cardboards or any leftover box and beautify it. On the inner side of the container with green ink draw the manifestation symbol and the image of your currency on one side, on the opposite side with red ink draw the CKR image. Towards the third end, make the Money Reiki image in blue ink and on the fourth end make the Dollar image and SHK in orange ink. Subsequently you can compose your monetary objectives for the year and put it in the crate and furthermore make different chits with your objectives and whatever else you want for instance: "I am getting loads of customers and making money consistently" or "I am purchasing a big house and living there joyfully with my family." Write them down like affirmations and after you place these in your case give it Reiki once in seven days while envisioning that your desires are getting shown.

4. Take a red shaded box or make a crate and stick a red paper on it and create designs on it. Place different kinds of Reiki images on it, which symbolize bounty, such as Midas Star, Vasudha and so on. Place a bit of pyrite alongside tumbles of citrine, aventurine, rose quartz and Merkabah crystals. Keep some cash in the box and try not to spend that money. Consistently at the end of every day, whatever little money is extra with you place it in that crate and continue adding cash to it day by day. You will discover heaps of money coming at you from all sources.

5. Creating a money magnet is a simple way of transforming an article into something that attracts money. Choose any object that is easy to carry with you every day. You can also wear it like jewelry or carry it like a crystal tumbler and transform it into your cash magnet. Take the article that you have chosen and purify it first with running water. Afterward, hold the item in the middle of your hands and speak out your goal boisterously as if you feel it occurring in your life for example "I am a cash magnet" or "I am pulling in cash from all sides." Then after this, charge that object with symbols of Money Reiki and other conventional Reiki images as well. You can also bless the article saying "I bless this item with the energy of money. May it help to acquire all of the wealth in my life, in my best interest, and in the interests of all others concerned. Thank you." Then you have to carry or wear this object with you wherever you go.

6. Take up your favorite energy circle, I'll post my energy circles, which I use additionally and sketch on each side the SHK, CKR and Money Reiki images, and it will upgrade the energies of the EC and help to pull in cash.

7. In Money Reiki, we have a great ace image which is an exceptionally groundbreaking image used to summon a lot of wealth. I do this on each Full Moon. I approach all Archangel Uriel, Michael and others up and furthermore call on Goddess Fortuna and Abundantia to clear me up of every one of my obligations and budgetary issues and envision the terrific ace image loop inside my entire body winding up and empowering me with cash energies. I imagine absorbing a green light while doing this.

8. A standout among the ideal approaches to get back wealth and a luxurious life endlessly is healing the world with Money Reiki. I initially sit for my meditation for this and afterward I envision the image of Mother Nature before me and ask for healing from Mother Nature with images of Money Reiki. I envision my Money Reiki setting off to all the needy individuals, the poor and the hungry in this entire world. Finally, I see the world upbeat, at peace and loaded up with affection and bounty. Along these lines when I favor Mother Nature with joy and wealth, that bounty returns to me in multiples.

9. Begin completing a self-healing session on all the chakras with Money Reiki images for ten minutes and after that envision cash and request pardoning for any pessimism you had towards cash and for all the negative blockages you have towards cash and discharge it to Mother Nature.

10. Create a different raised area for abundance in your meditation room and in the table place images or statues of goddess Fortuna, Lakshmi and Lord Ganesha with five bits of pyrites and a container of pyramid shape, and green light. Absorb the green flame day by day and give Money Reiki to the raised area and part with some level of your profit each month in this pyramid box. When a year has passed, gather the cash from the crate and spend it on nourishing the homeless individuals or stray creatures. A standout among the ideal approaches to build salary is separating a level of it in the pyramid box, as pyramids will duplicate what you put in it.

Using these tips will help you bring in prosperity this coming year and those in the future as well.

Chapter Six :

Affirmations for Prosperity

In the basic terms, the meaning of affirmations (now and then called "self-insistences") is utilizing 'positive sentences that you repeat to yourself' to develop faith in yourself and in the subliminal personality. This implies viably composing a rundown of affirmations that rouse and spur you to be better and help to conquer internal limitations and self-doubt.

When you first begin saying these expressions, they may not really be valid. Be that as it may, they ought to be intended to reflect what you need to be valid. You have to make them incredible and one of a kind to who and what you need them to turn into. At that point, after some time, the constant reiteration of day-by-day positive affirmations will reshape your inward convictions and suspicions about yourself and your general surroundings. This reshaping gives you a progressively positive impression of your identity and where you stand. So above all, you need to really trust an assertion to be valid.

As indicated by the Law of Attraction, what you think and feel shapes your world. The intensity of attestations lies in their capacity to change your outer world by first changing your interior one. Moreover, you can utilize affirmations for a wide range of objectives, from self-assurance to vocation achievement, love, and plenitude. Their solitary constraints are the ones you place on them.

Research on this demonstrates that when you're focused on something, you can help your critical thinking aptitudes by utilizing self-affirmations. Along these lines, affirmations can enable you to perform better under strain. This is especially helpful in circumstances like prospective employee meetings and first dates!

Day by day repeating affirmations will help you in gaining wealth, as opposed to needing it. This can enable you to manifest your Law of Attraction objectives at a much quicker rate.

Affirmations make you increasingly mindful of your manner of thinking. More noteworthy mindfulness makes you bound to challenge negative musings as they emerge. This additionally upgrades your sense of self-realization, improving how you comprehend what you truly need throughout everyday life.

Positive assertions reconnect you with sentiments of appreciation and improve your point of view on the beneficial things throughout everyday life. This can help you achieve bliss, just as your vibrational energy becomes more positive.

Ongoing exploration shows that hopeful individuals will, in general, have better cardiovascular wellbeing. So if your affirmations make you progressively hopeful, they could assist you with living longer as well.

In outline, self-affirmations are useful for your body and spiritual well being. Truth be told, numerous individuals use them even when they don't work effectively at times. By changing the manner in which you think, they can push you to gradually change as long as you can remember to practice this and think this way every day.

If you want to harness the law of attraction for money, you need to use the right affirmations in order to keep your mind focused and on your goals. The following are some simple and effective phrases that will help you attract wealth and abundance in life.

1. Money is good, and I love money.
2. I will attract more money every single day.
3. I am successful and live a joyful life.

4. I can attract an unlimited amount of wealth.

5. I can succeed in attracting wealth and achieving any goals I set.

6. I know the value of money and am grateful for all that I receive.

7. It is easy for me to earn money.

8. I will always have more money than I need.

9. I am a magnet for wealth and abundance.

Using these affirmations in various exercises will help you to manifest your intentions faster.

Conclusion

As you come to the end of this book, I would like to thank you for investing your time in reading it. I hope you found it resourceful. You can see how vast the scope of energy healing is in your life if you keep an open mind. There is so much you can manifest in your life with the help of this. Stop worrying about where your money will come from or if you will ever be wealthy.

If you think negatively and allow negative energy to enter your life, it will result in negative manifestations. However, if you start thinking and believing in positive outcomes, they will surely manifest in your life. You can try energy healing and bring in prosperity and happiness for yourself and your loved ones.

If you found this book useful, you can even recommend it to friends or family who might need it. Energy healing is universally effective, and there's so much more to explore than what you have learned here.

And finally, if you liked the book, I would like to ask you to do me a favor and leave a review for the book on Amazon. Just go to your account on Amazon or click on the link below.

LEAVE A REVIEW ON AMAZON!

Thank you and good luck!

References

https://reikirays.com/29487/ways-to-prosperity-with-money-reiki/
http://www.thelawofattraction.com/what-is-the-law-of-attraction/
https://www.thesecret.tv/law-of-attraction/
https://www.jackcanfield.com/blog/using-the-law-of-attraction/
https://www.mindbodygreen.com/0-23890/what-everyone-should-know-about-energy-healing.html
https://deborahking.com/topics/energy-healing/
https://www.asbestos.com/treatment/alternative/energy-therapies/

www.ingramcontent.com/pod-product-compliance
Lightning Source LLC
Chambersburg PA
CBHW021933170526
45157CB00005B/2298

9 781098 703417